Monster Science

ZOMBIES AND ELECTRICITY

BY MARK WEAKLAND • ILLUSTRATED BY JOK

Consultant:
Joanne K. Olson, PhD
Associate Professor, Science Education
Iowa State University
Ames, Iowa

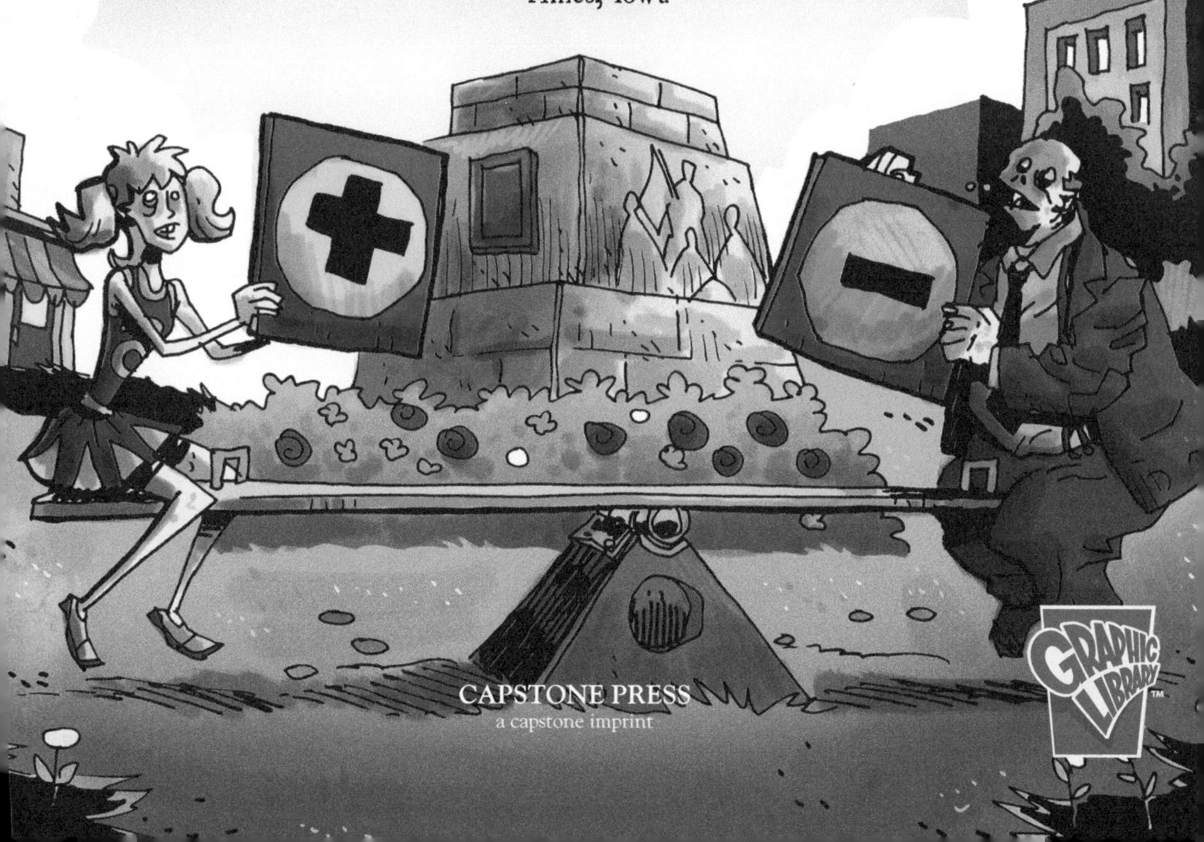

CAPSTONE PRESS
a capstone imprint

GRAPHIC LIBRARY™

Graphic Library is published by Capstone Press,
1710 Roe Crest Drive, North Mankato, Minnesota 56003
www.capstonepub.com

Library of Congress Cataloging-in-Publication Data
Cataloging-in-publication information is on file with the Library of Congress.
ISBN 978-1-4296-9929-7 (hardcover)
ISBN 978-1-62065-822-2 (paperback)
ISBN 978-1-4765-1593-9 (eBook PDF)

Editor
Anthony Wacholtz

Designer
Alison Thiele

Art Director
Nathan Gassman

Production Specialist
Laura Manthe

Printed in the United States
5999

TABLE OF
CONTENTS

CHAPTER 1

ELECTRIC ZOMBIES

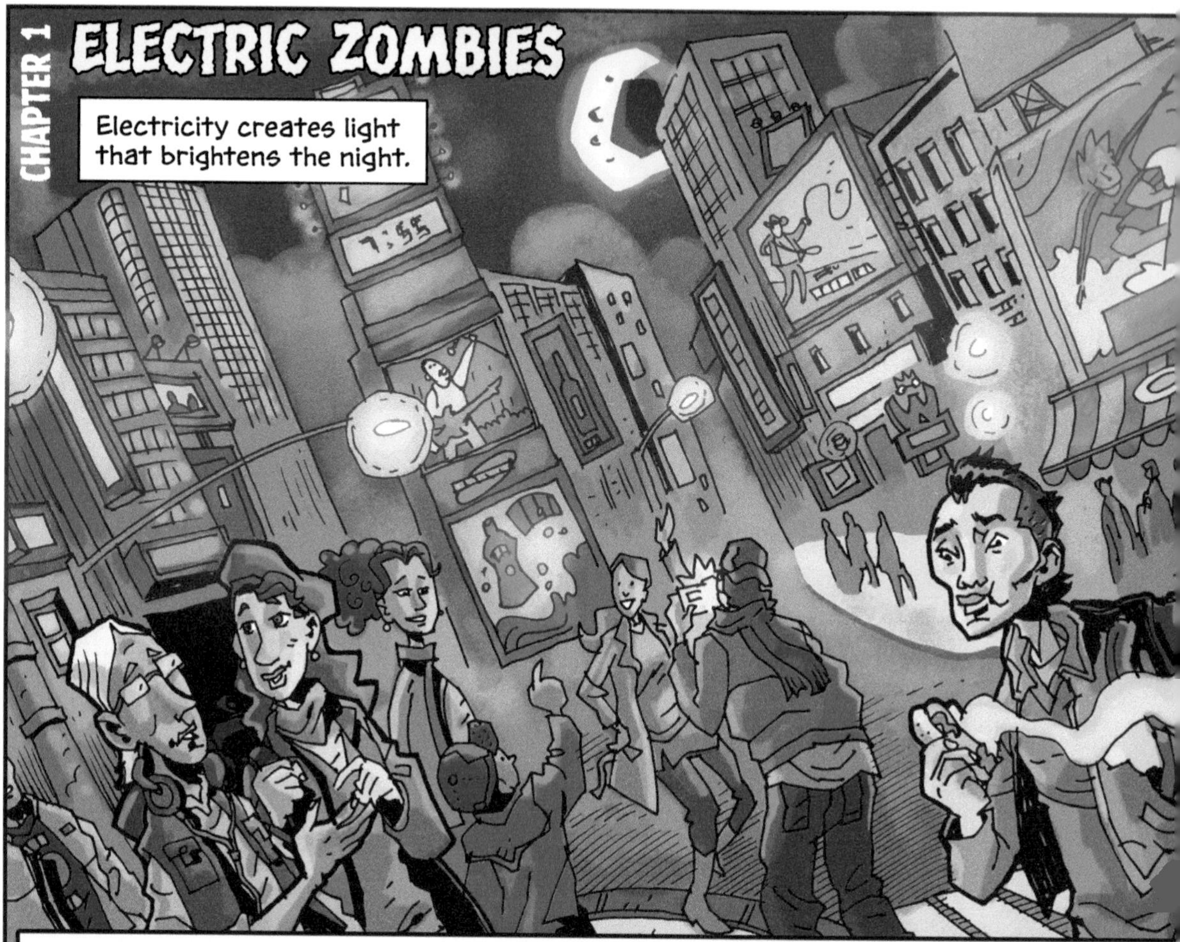
Electricity creates light that brightens the night.
7:55

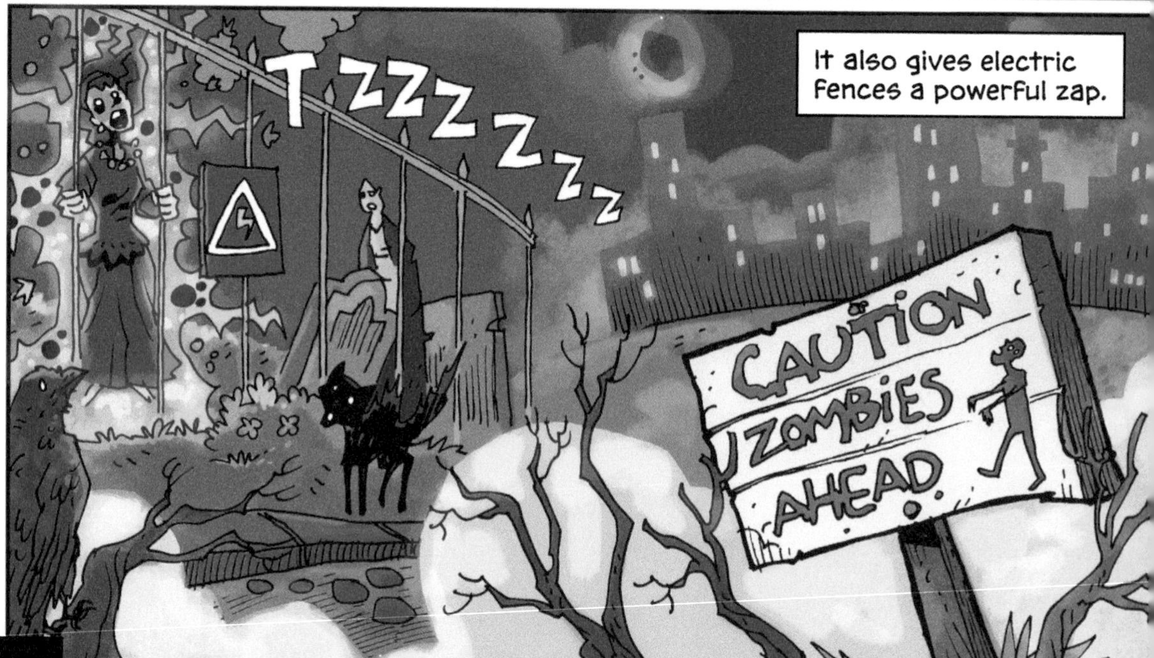
It also gives electric fences a powerful zap.
TZZZZZZZ
CAUTION
ZOMBIES
AHEAD

But electricity does more than power lights and electrify fences. It runs hair driers, toasters, computers, televisions, and more.

We depend on electricity day and night. Turn off the electricity and many things stop working. But what exactly is electricity? And how does it work?

CHAPTER 2

CHARGE!

To understand electricity, you must first understand atoms. Atoms are the building blocks of nature. Prunes, the moon, helium balloons—they're all made of atoms.

BRAINS?

Yes, brains are made of atoms too.

TEENY TINY ATOMS

It's almost impossible to understand the size of one atom. But try pinching this page between your thumb and pointer finger. The thickness of one book page equals about one million atoms lined up end to end.

Atoms are the smallest part of any substance. Imagine you find a zombie's gold tooth. A gold tooth is made of billions and billions of gold atoms.

While atoms are small, tinier particles make up atoms. Protons, neutrons, and electrons are the three basic particles that make up an atom. Protons and neutrons are bundled together in the atom's nucleus. Electrons move within an electron cloud around the nucleus, like wasps madly buzzing around a nest.

BZZZZ

NEUTRON

ELECTRON CLOUD

PROTON

NUCLEUS

ELECTRON

Electrons and protons have a charge.

CHARGE!

No, not that kind of charge. Instead, a charge can be thought of as a force, like a push or a pull. Protons have a positive charge. Electrons have a negative charge. Neutrons are neutral. They have no charge at all.

An atom is full of negative and positive charges. However, its overall charge is neutral. Why? The negative charge of its electrons is balanced by the positive charge of its protons.

Electrons usually stay with their atoms. However, electrons can be made to leave one atom and jump to another. When this happens, both atoms become charged.

When electrons make the jump between atoms through certain materials, such as air or metal, electricity is created.

CHAPTER 3

ZOMBIES AND CURRENT EVENTS

Electricity can travel through solids and liquids. It can also move through the air.

BZZZ

When electricity travels through solids and liquids, such as metal and water, it's called current.

current—a flow of electrons through an object

10

Just like a river is a flow of water, a current is a flow of electrons.

A river current flows along a riverbed. Electric current typically flows through a metal wire.

Electrons in metal are not tightly bound to their atoms. They easily jump from one metal atom to another. Most power lines use copper wire to carry electricity from one place to another.

11

Static electricity is electricity moving through the air. It is produced when objects rub together, pass electrons, and become charged. One object has a positive charge. The other has a negative charge.

Meeowww

The positive and negative charges of atoms push and pull each other. These forces are similar to how magnets push (repel) and pull (attract) with magnetic force.

SORRY, BUT I'M NOT ATTRACTED.

static electricity—the buildup of electrical charges on the surface of an object; static electricity can be created by friction

Consider a zombie dressed in a wool shirt lurching against a bunch of balloons. When the zombie brushes the balloons, negatively charged electrons move from the wool shirt to the balloons.

BRAINS?

BALLOONS!

ZOMBIE BALOON

The wool now has a positive charge, and the balloons have a negative charge. The negatively and positively charged atoms attract one another. That's why the balloons cling to the shirt.

NATURAL ELECTRICITY

Lightning is a huge discharge of static electricity. Negative charges in the clouds are attracted to the positively charged ground, creating lightning. Bolts of lightning can travel at speeds up to 130,000 miles (210,000 kilometers) per hour, and their temperatures can hit nearly 54,000 degrees Fahrenheit (30,000 degrees Celsius).

Electric current flows in a continuous path from the source of the electricity, through the wire and any other devices, and back to the source. This loop is called a circuit.

On a model railroad, a circle of train track forms a simple circuit. The train wheels pick up electricity from the track, making the engine's electric motor turn.

CHUFF CHUFF

A power source pushes current around the circuit. Electricity flows around the track as long as the circuit is unbroken. If there is a gap in the track, the circuit is broken. The train engine stops.

circuit—the continuous path of an electrical current

Many circuits include a switch. When a switch is open, the circuit is broken. The electric current stops flowing around the track and the train stops.

FIX TRACK FOR BRAINS?

When the switch is closed, the circuit is complete. Electric current flows through the continuous path of metal, and the train runs once more.

Electricity flows along paths provided by other types of metals too. Both aluminum and steel are pathways for electricity. Liquids such as water or battery acid also provide paths for electricity.

ZTTT

LOOKS LIKE WE'VE GOT A PROBLEM.

YOU CAN SAY THAT AGAIN!

Metal, water, and acids are good conductors. Conductors are materials through which electricity flows.

conductor—a substance that allows electricity to pass through it

16

On the other hand, some materials are good insulators. Insulators block the flow of electricity. Good insulators include wood, glass, rubber, and plastic. Seat foam, fabric, and rubber tires insulate and protect people inside a car.

B..B...R...A..I... N...S...S...?

A SHOCKING DISCOVERY

Ben Franklin's famous kite experiment in 1752 gave evidence that lightning is electricity. After the experiment, Franklin invented lightning rods, which are conductors. When lightning strikes the rods, the strong electrical current is grounded.

COULD YOU HOLD THIS?

insulator—a substance that prevents or reduces the passage of electricity
ground—to safely pass electricity into the earth

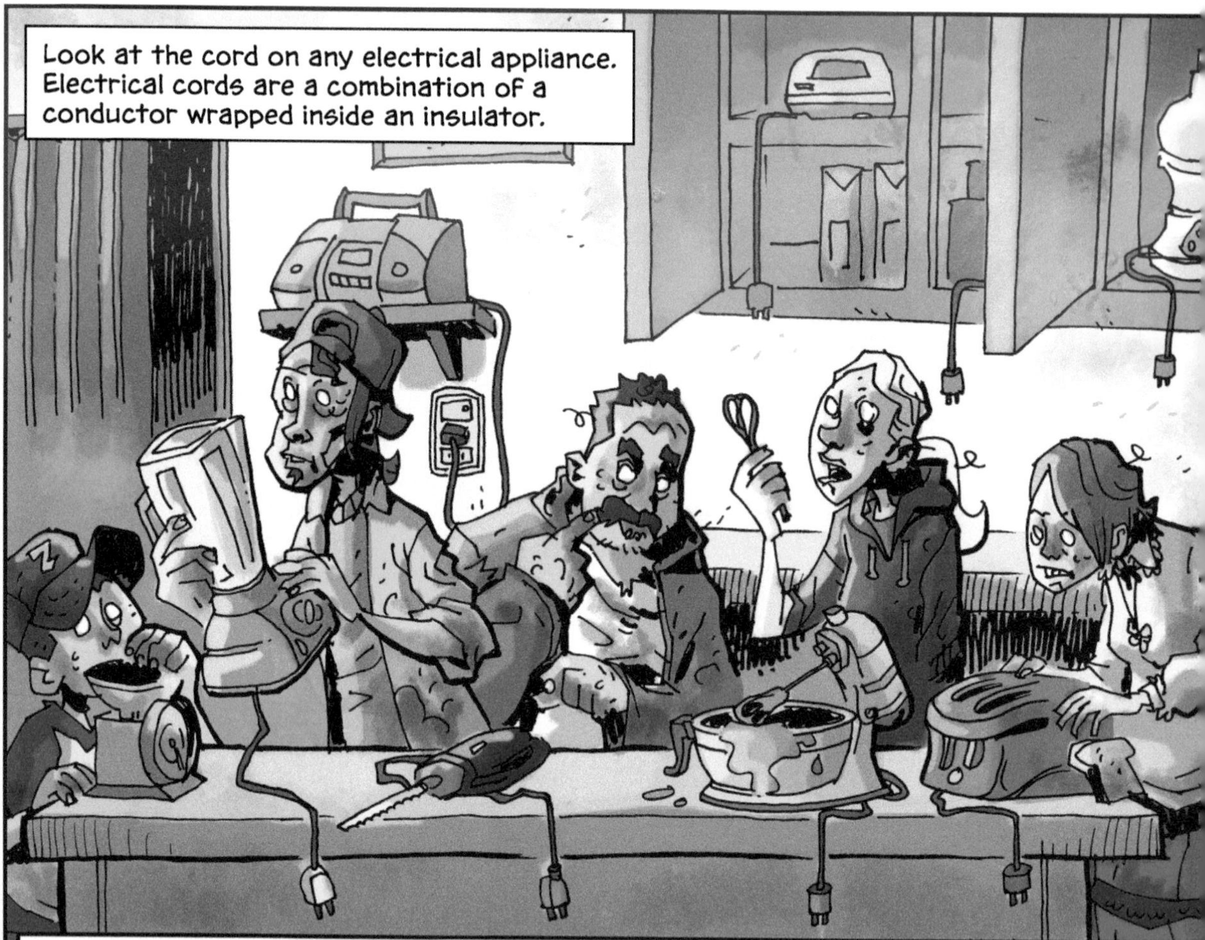
Look at the cord on any electrical appliance. Electrical cords are a combination of a conductor wrapped inside an insulator.

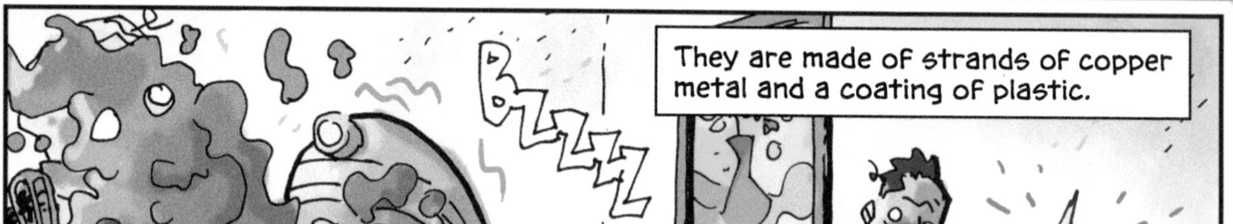
They are made of strands of copper metal and a coating of plastic.
BZZZZZ
CONDUCTOR
INSULATOR

For wires that carry more power, strands of aluminum may be used. Once again, a plastic coating insulates the wire.

In all wires and electrical cords, metal is a pathway for flowing electrons. The plastic coating blocks the electrons from escaping.

OOOH!

BZZZZ

AAAH!

CHAPTER 4

PUSH, PULL, AND POWER PLANTS

The positive and negative charges of atoms act like the positive and negative forces of a magnet. The relationship between electricity and magnetism is called electromagnetism.

Electricity can be used to create a magnet. Start with a thick coil of wire. Then send electricity through the coil. As electric current flows, magnetic force is created. It's an electromagnet!

BMMMM

BRAINS!

More coils means more magnetic force. So does passing more electricity through the wires. Therefore, using more coils and electricity will result in a stronger magnet.

Unlike regular magnets, electromagnets can be turned on and off.

Around the world, electricity flows through miles and miles of wires. Where does all this electricity come from? How is it made? The answer is power plants, also known as generating stations.

To generate electricity, power plants start with an energy source. Most power plants burn fossil fuels such as natural gas or coal.

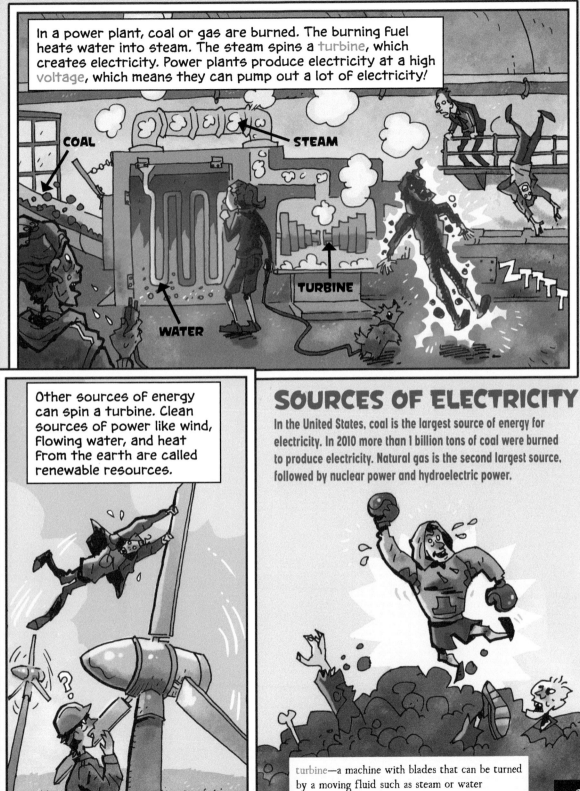

In a power plant, coal or gas are burned. The burning fuel heats water into steam. The steam spins a turbine, which creates electricity. Power plants produce electricity at a high voltage, which means they can pump out a lot of electricity!

COAL

STEAM

TURBINE

WATER

Other sources of energy can spin a turbine. Clean sources of power like wind, flowing water, and heat from the earth are called renewable resources.

SOURCES OF ELECTRICITY

In the United States, coal is the largest source of energy for electricity. In 2010 more than 1 billion tons of coal were burned to produce electricity. Natural gas is the second largest source, followed by nuclear power and hydroelectric power.

turbine—a machine with blades that can be turned by a moving fluid such as steam or water
voltage—the force of an electric current

23

The shaft of the spinning turbine is connected to a generator. Generators are the machines that create electricity. They are made up of magnets and coils of wire.

GENERATOR

The shaft coming from the turbine connects to giant magnets. These magnets sit inside an even larger sleeve of coiled wire. When the shaft turns, the magnets turn. As the magnets turn inside the coiled wire, electrons begin to jump from one atom to another.

MAGNET

MAKES ELECTRICITY, NOT BRAINS ...

generator—a machine used to convert mechanical energy, the energy of motion, into electricity

Bigger magnets, more wire, and a faster spin all cause more and more electrons to jump and flow.

OOOOOOOH!

Trillions of flowing electrons create electric current. The current flows from the power plant into huge power lines. The power lines then carry the electricity to homes and businesses everywhere.

DIRECT CURRENT

ALTERNATING CURRENT

AC VS. DC

Electricity generated in a power plant is called alternating current (AC). Alternating current flows back and forth. It reverses itself 60 times each second. Direct current (DC) flows in only one direction. Batteries are one source of direct current.

CHAPTER 5

SAFE FROM ZAPPING, SAFE FROM ZOMBIES

When electrons escape from a broken cord, electricity is lost. More importantly, a defective power cord is dangerous. The cord's plastic coating protects anyone holding it. Its insulation keeps flowing electrons away from a sensitive conductor—your skin!

Flesh is a good conductor of electricity. If a zombie grabs an uninsulated wire, it WILL get zapped. If you grabbed that cord, you'd get zapped too. So use your brains and be careful!

ZAPP

ZAPPP

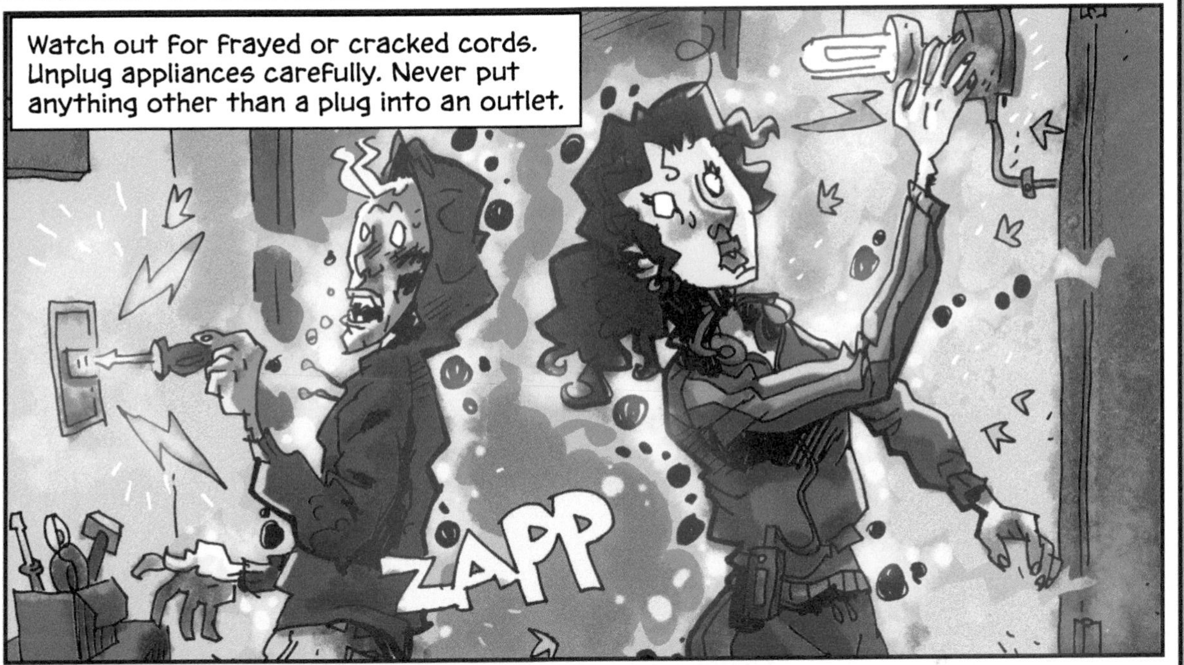
Watch out for frayed or cracked cords. Unplug appliances carefully. Never put anything other than a plug into an outlet.
ZAPP

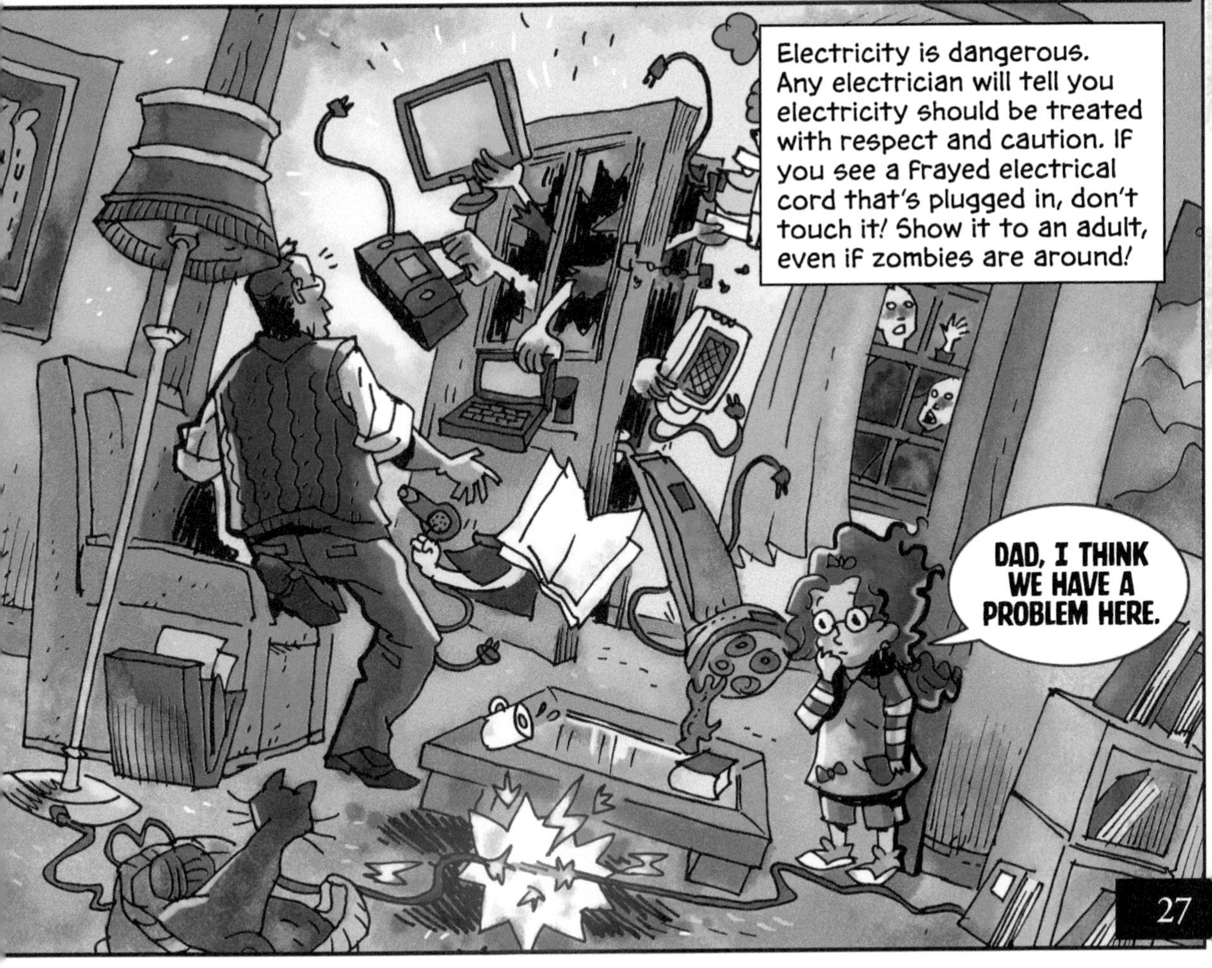
Electricity is dangerous. Any electrician will tell you electricity should be treated with respect and caution. If you see a frayed electrical cord that's plugged in, don't touch it! Show it to an adult, even if zombies are around!
DAD, I THINK WE HAVE A PROBLEM HERE.

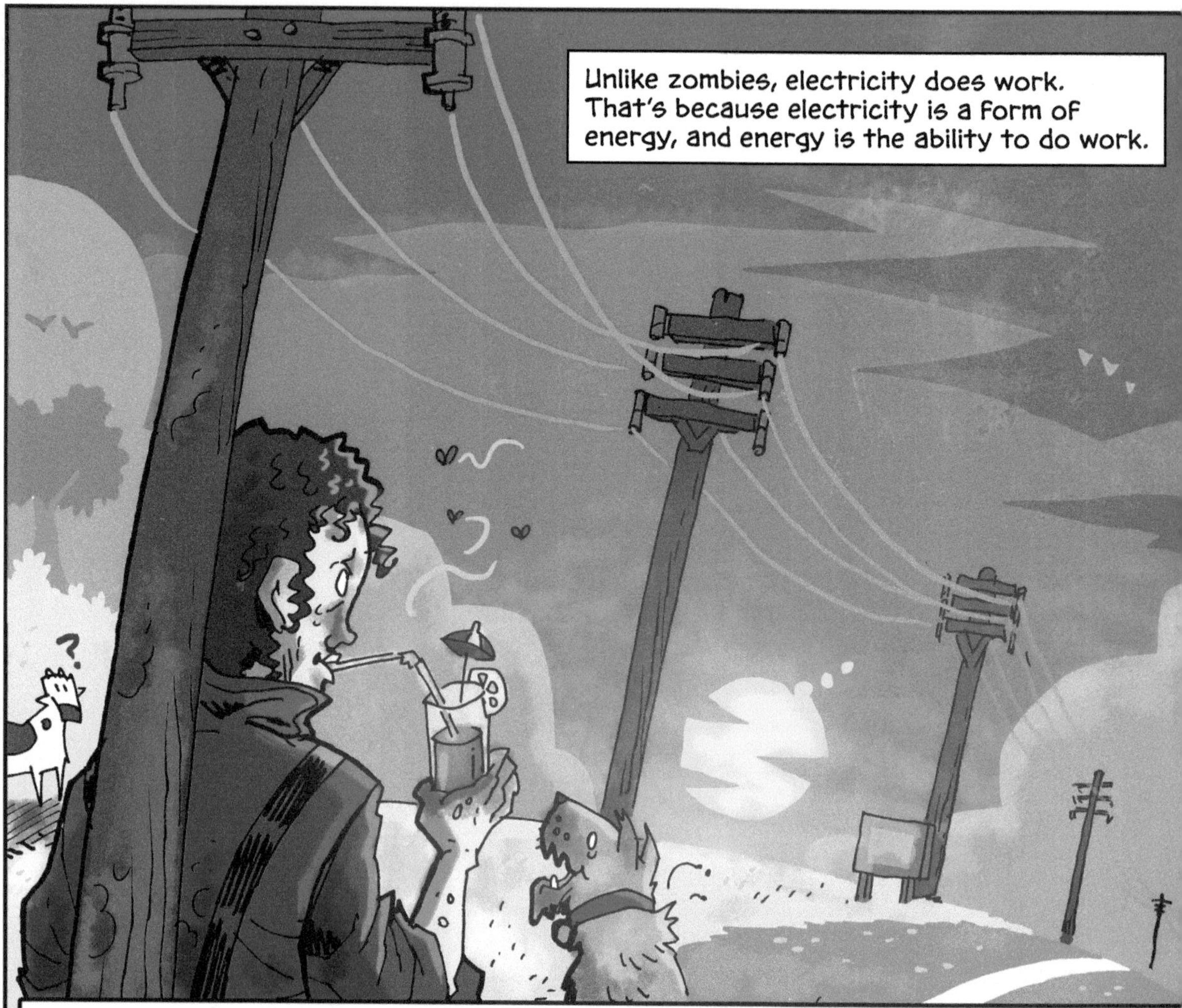
Unlike zombies, electricity does work. That's because electricity is a form of energy, and energy is the ability to do work.

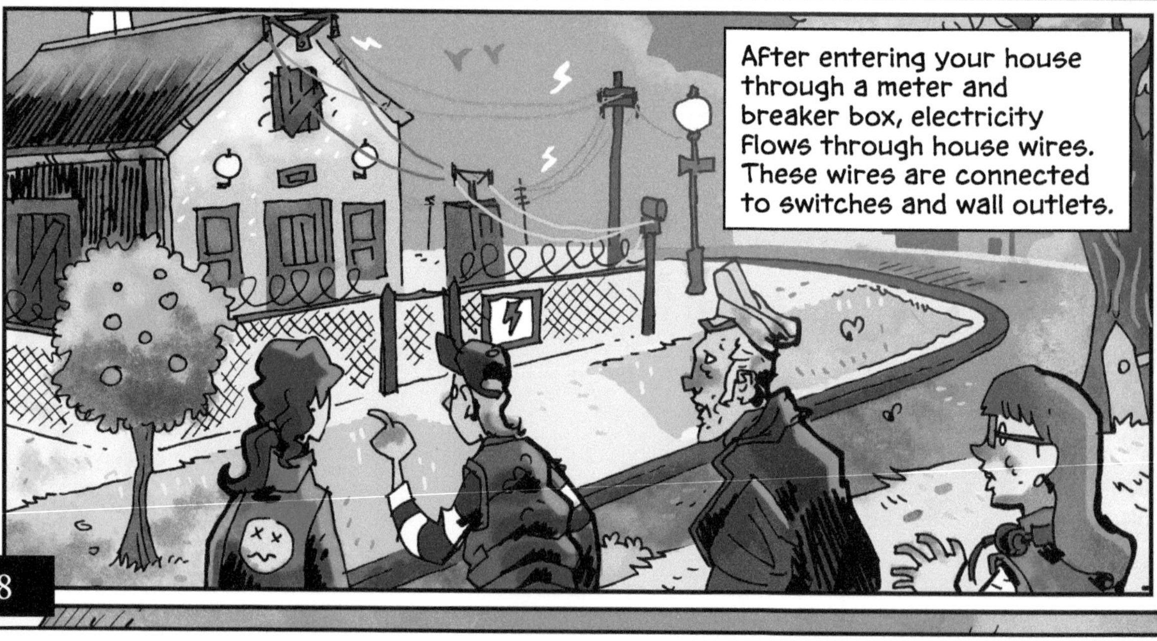
After entering your house through a meter and breaker box, electricity flows through house wires. These wires are connected to switches and wall outlets.

Electricity powers the electric motors that spin in vacuums and blenders. It heats the coils on your stove and energizes the magnets in a microwave. All you have to do is plug in the appliances, push a button, and let electricity do the work for you.

Electricity instantly turns on the lights and powers the electric fence. Aren't you glad you have it in your life?

GLOSSARY

charge (CHARJ)—a property of subatomic particles, such as protons and electrons, that can be positive or negative

circuit (SUHR-kuht)—the complete path of an electrical current

conductor (kuhn-DUHK-tuhr)—a substance that allows electricity to pass along it or through it

current (KUHR-uhnt)—a flow of electrons through an object

electromagnet (i-lek-troh-MAG-nuht)—a temporary magnet created when an electric current flows through a conductor

generator (JEN-uh-ray-tur)—a machine used to convert mechanical energy into electricity

ground (GROUND)—to safely pass electricity into the earth

insulator (IN-suh-late-ur)—a substance that prevents or reduces the passage of electricity

static electricity (STAH-tik i-lek-TRISS-uh-tee)—the buildup of an electrical charge on the surface of an object

turbine (TUR-bine)—a machine with blades that can be turned by a moving fluid such as steam or water

voltage (VOHL-tij)—the force of an electric current

READ MORE

O'Donnell, Liam. *The Shocking World of Electricity with Max Axiom, Super Scientist.* Graphic Science. Mankato, Minn.: Capstone Press, 2007.

Solway, Andrew. *Generating and Using Electricity.* Why Science Matters. Chicago: Heinemann Library, 2009.

Walker, Sally M. *Investigating Electricity.* How Does Energy Work? Minneapolis: Lerner Publications, 2012.

INTERNET SITES

FactHound offers a safe, fun way to find Internet sites related to this book. All sites on FactHound have been researched by our staff.

Here's all you do:

Visit *www.facthound.com*

Type in this code: 9781429699297

Super-cool stuff!

Check out projects, games and lots more at
www.capstonekids.com

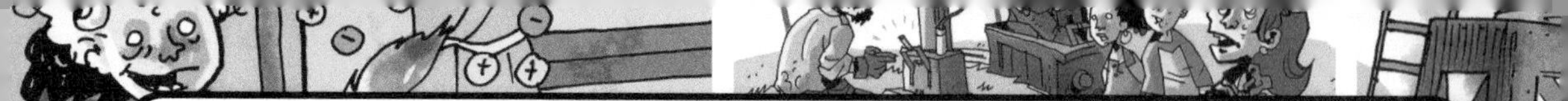

INDEX

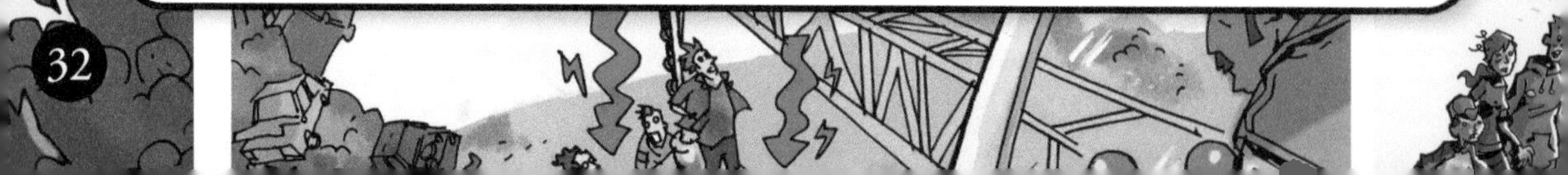